DON'T JUDGE ME

PJ Edmund

SWEEDIE
GERALD
PUBLISHING HOUSE
A SUBSIDIARY OF PJ EDMUND MINISTRIES

Copyright © 2018 PJ Edmund

All rights reserved.

ISBN-10:1717319076
ISBN-13:978-1717319074

DEDICATION

To my parents Bishops Gerald and Sweedie Edmund for everything you deposited even when I didn't know it, continue to rest in Glory! I continue to do what I do through your example and legacy.

CONTENTS

	Acknowledgments	i
1	How could this happen?	9
2	Facing the Haters	18
3	Someone Needs to Get Me	23
4	Vulnerable	32
5	Private Session	35
6	This Turned Out Very Differently	42

ACKNOWLEDGMENTS

My family has always been an amazing source of support and inspiration. To my wife Chelly for all the prayers. To my children PJ , Jr., Britanny Chantelle, Eryka Christine and Miche Shanice.
To my brother Bishop Dexter Edmund, my sisters Hedy Christine, Geraldine Shandylane, Deborath Ruth (rest in Glory!), and Rachel Rose. We have come through it all together!
. I am grateful for the editing and proof reading support on this project of Lisa Fields, Rashida Griffin and Denize Shy.

1 HOW COULD THIS HAPPEN?

Where do I begin and how do I begin to explain my life? I have a name, but because of my lifestyle I'm simply referred to as woman! I'm not sure how to explain how I ended up here. I'm not proud to be here as this place does not describe or define the true me. I would love to say that I was proud of this place but that would not be accurate. My life was generally normal, but good. I remember growing up with wonderful days of fun filled family laughter, days passed with innocent adventure. We had a large family with cousins that virtually lived in the next community. I've always found enjoyment in friendships and relationships and generally I was marginally popular because I was fun to be around. I grew up in a household with both my parents. They appeared to genuinely love and care for each other. My parents ensured that my siblings and I were raised with a good work ethic through daily chores around the house, making sure we all participated in the upkeep of the family and contributing to the general running of the home. With all the great and wonderful aspects of my life I sadly remember feeling vividly alone much of the time, desperate and needy but not knowing why something was missing. I grew up not realizing we were poor. There always seemed to be enough food to go around and virtually everyone in our neighborhood had the same level of living. I had no idea the kind of pain and dysfunction that was lurking in the corners of my beautifully fabricated life. I knew at times I desired life to be better and always recalled youthful dreams of doing something incredible, lasting and significant. I never knew where that dream or desire came from. Important was not how you would describe anyone in my family I learnt, but I felt that something important was going to happen to me. My mother guided us the best way she could but always told me that I needed a man in my life to get ahead, a man she felt would give me meaning and purpose. I should not have been surprised, when I ended up in the situation I'm in now because of a man!

I have a secret that I have kept to myself. It's not easy to share but I feel, to be honest, this is my time to share it. This thing that I am getting ready to tell you has got to be the most embarrassing thing I have ever done. Since we are being honest, this has got to be the most embarrassing thing I have ever been caught doing. It still baffles me why there was so much attention centered on today. It had been an ordinary day for me, filled with the usual dose of desperation and unhappiness. In the outside world the sun shone radiantly on everything in its path, the wind blew gently, the sky majestically covered everything as far as the eye could see. These days seemed to come and go with no hurried schedule. Every day seemed to be the same, the sun rises and the moon sets and life wanders aimlessly on like a well-thought-out calendar. When you feel as desperate as I have been feeling lately, every day seems longer and more depressing than the day before. You can see how I could easily end up thinking, feeling and absolutely doing desperate, helpless, lonely things. The desperate thoughts that fill your mind when there is nothing else to occupy it is frightening. I really had no reason to be with this man today. I knew it was not right, and yes, my woman's intuition kicked in just like any other day, week, month or year. I don't remember who introduced me to this opportunity, but I had seen these people many times around the community. It was always these kinds of men that wanted to pay for time with me. These men lived double lives, ridiculously respectable by day and despicably appalling by night. They knew I was desperate. How do men discern that in us? These men tended to specialize in the manipulation of desperate women, trying their best to make life better. Something was odd about the way they hurriedly forced me out of my house into this strange house. There was a man constantly promising me that all my personal and financial needs would be met. You cannot say that to desperate people. You should not say that to me, not today. Honestly, I was excited about what was developing, even though something in me sensed that this was either going to be the beginning of something great or something disastrous. With all my premonitions, thoughts and emotions racing through my head, I still went inside the house!

Immediately after entering the house I felt uneasy and unsettled. I didn't feel right. I was nervous. The house was dark and scantily lit, scantily furnished and generally gave off the feeling of depravity. Whoever lived here would have had to live in a climate of despair. Perhaps no one lived here at all. I wondered if this is where these guys brought other women like me. I kept telling myself to turn around and run. I should have done just that. I should have tried with everything in me to escape. It is incredible how paralyzed you feel when you realize you are trapped. All I really felt good at throughout my whole life was fulfilling other people's desires and allowing everything and anything to control me. I feel helpless and hopeless! I know this feeling needs to end, I am aware of that, but that's not where I am today. I am pretty sure it won't end today. Foolishly, I followed these men into an isolated part of the house. I am surrounded by strange men, strange energy and strange sensations, but still here I am. I know this is not the answer, and I don't want this, but I can't stop. Why do I still feel the need to stay here?

My worst fears were confirmed. I knew these men were too eager to hustle me into this part of the house where another man was laying down. Don't get me wrong, I would not normally be opposed to arrangements like this, but this time it felt different. Sadly, most of these men I already knew. This situation seemed to unfold so slowly and deliberately in front of me with no apparent regard for the impact it would have on me. I looked quickly into their empty and futureless faces that reflected the same emptiness in my own contorted life. They looked frantic, excited and anxious. They never really spoke to me just gestured as to what they wanted me to do. The person laying down was a new man. I had never seen him before. He looked as frantic, confused and anxious as I did. He did not seem to want to be here either. This situation was getting weirder by the second. Why were they forcing us together? What was the real reason for this connection? I looked carelessly around the sparsely lit room, familiar with the dark, but unfamiliar with what I was sensing. The atmosphere is very different now. I can hardly breath trying to remain focused on all that was happening. My heart beat was agonizingly fast like it was getting ready to explode. I still wanted out from this place no matter how much money they promised me. I wish I had really thought this through. I could have, would have, should have tried harder to escape. This time I did not want to give myself away, not this time at least!

As I turned to try and find a route of escape, one of the men struck me brutally in the back of my head. Of course, I've been hit and beaten before, but this strike was vicious. It was a crushing blow that made my escape now impossible. I felt dizzy and in my concussed state, I still look around trying to find a possible opening to stumble through. This was not going to be good for me, I could feel the walls closing in making me a permanent prisoner to my choice. My head was swirling, my thoughts were confused, and nothing seemed to make sense. I remember how the blood gushed down my back and I heard myself release a cry that even scared me. As a mother, I am extremely intuitive about cries. I know the cry of a child who is hungry, a child who is annoyed and a child who is tired. There is a different cry when a child is in pain. This cry that I heard emanating from deep inside me signaled extreme pain and desperation. This is not turning out to be the opportunity that I thought it would be. This was a coerced and planned event and I still was no wiser as to what it was all about. No sooner had my head savagely hit the floor that I felt these men mercilessly rip the very clothes off my back. I spin around quickly in total disbelief. I have heard the gripping tales of so many women in my village who have been the victims of this kind of abuse. They tell the gory details of the animalistic urges they have been subjected to by men who have little regard for women or life. I cannot believe this is happening to me. Panic sets in and even in my delirious state, I try pathetically to fight back with everything in me. I struggle and wrestle with these men who I knew were more powerful than I was. I cannot just let this happen without defending what was left of my fading honor. This is unfair and deplorable. If I decide to contract with a man, it's my choice! This is not an agreement, this is an absolute violation of me. I desperately tried to blindly snatch back my clothes in an attempt to cover myself. It was too late. I was already exposed and unprotected from the onslaught of this forced and painful act. No matter where I tried to turn I was met with the same level of aggression. I am no saint, I have had my share of physical altercations before and I know how to handle myself. I have been both the aggressor and the defender. This time I am literally fighting for my life. The torrent of hits and kicks and blows rain down on me like a tsunami. No part of my body is spared the savagery of abrasions and bruises. What have I done to deserve this kind of unprovoked attack? Maybe this is payment for my past indiscretions, and if that is the case then I may not get out of this alive. The beating which seemed to last forever has stopped now but this relentless assault has made me powerless to fight what was coming next.

I felt ashamed, but what was I feeling ashamed of? It wasn't as if I had not done this before! This time was so different though. I felt different about it. The man who I had been hired for this arrangement, looked hopelessly into my eyes not seeming to enjoy what was happening either. Maybe this too was not what he had entirely bargained for. The onlookers were jeering, yelling and inciting this man to violate someone he didn't even know. His eyes seemed apologetic, they appeared to be filled with remorse, pity even. Why were they doing this to me? If I didn't have to feed the mouths in my house, I would never have agreed to be here in the first place. This was the only way I knew. I had no other choice, and even with my life hanging in the balance, I am sacrificing my own dignity, to do for my family, that I know in my heart they may not do for me. They did not rip his clothes off! Here I am in the middle of nowhere, surrounded by frenzied men completely at their mercy with no one to call on. I screamed anyhow. I hope someone hears my frantic plea for help and does something. I do need to be rescued, I admit it. I have gotten myself into something that is way out of my depths. I'm only to blame. I thought I agreed to earn some money, but I did not choose what's happening to me right now.

For what could only be described as a period of several hours, I was subjected to the worst kind of physical and emotional debauchery I have ever experienced. Most of what happened to me I cannot fully recall because of loss of consciousness. I was completely brutalized, completely mesmerized by a level of treatment that no human should ever experience. When I came out of my state of unconsciousness the room was completely dark, subdued and filled with an overpowering oppressive atmosphere. Anyone walking into this room would immediately sense what had just happened here. The air reeked of violence, the savagery that I had just survived. Without warning, one of the men grab me from behind barely giving me enough time to grab some of my clothes. They dragged me out of the house, pulling me ungraciously and unceremoniously by my hair while calling me disgraceful names and accusing me of violating some law. All I could hear while being dragged in the dirt were conversations of what these men believed would happen to me. I was not violating the law at all! If anything, these men manipulated the violation through this pre-arranged situation. Any other time I would have justified what happened in this room because I had a family to feed. This time everything went wrong because it was not the invitation I thought it was. My body is my product. I am not proud that this is the lifestyle that I was forced into, but with a husband that could not provide for his family, because of a disability, this is what I have to do. I did not choose this lifestyle, it chose me. There are other women in my village secretly involved in a similar lifestyle, yet why was I singled out? There is something more to this situation, I know it!

Friends and neighbors line the street as I am dragged through my own community. My eyes are swollen and virtually closed because of the beating I have taken. I barely see the faces of disgust. People are shaking their heads and whispering to each other as I pass by. How quickly people can change towards you when they do not know the entire story? I fear my side of this story will never be told. I am a woman in a man-controlled world. There is no way that I will be able to come out of this unscathed. I am already trapped in a system that is stacked against me. These people cannot make me feel any less than what I already feel. My shame is compounded by the discrimination that line the streets to wherever we are going. I pray my children do not see me this way. I pray my husband does not see me this way. Why are they doing this to me, this is not fair? I hear these men talking about another man, some stranger, a great and important man that will fix this whole situation. They know him, but I have yet to meet him. So, is that what this is about? I don't want anyone to meet me for the first time like this, not looking like this. What will he think of me when he sees me this way? I really want to end this embarrassing parade. There are people in my community that know how I earn my living, but I don't want the whole world to know! The stranger is constantly being mentioned. I am a part of this, but this stranger is the reason for this. They mention his name too often. What is their fascination with this stranger, I have got to know? What was an overcast and gloomy day suddenly seemed to brighten momentarily when this stranger is mentioned. For just a moment, I look up and discover something other than pity peering back at me. The sun smiled for an instant, and the clouds whitened momentarily and maybe, just maybe that ray of sunlight suggests that although things look bad for me, maybe hope is also here. I was in no position to argue. I took that as a sign for me!

Why are they taking me to this stranger? What does he have to do with all of this? I'm beginning to think this is more about him and less about me. I just don't know how? This has got to be the worst day of my life. I cannot think of another situation that I've been in that has made me feel like this. I've been humiliated before, but never like this. I've been abused before by countless men, but never like this. The only real hope I have right now is possibly this stranger that appears to be so important and powerful. I am feeling that he is going to be a different kind of man. I can only hope that he is kind and generous for some crazy reason. I am putting my hope in a stranger. I can hear them strategizing and planning what they are going to say to him. Wait a minute! This is sounding more and more like a trap, like a set up. The worse thing is they are using me to do it I think. I've been used many times before but never like this. I feel like a pawn in a game of uncaring chess, not knowing how I am going to be moved and used to ultimately win. I was not selected for my worth or for my influence. I am no one. I am just an average woman with little notoriety, little prestige, and little significance at all. I am still trying to process what led to the choice to pick me out for this sadistic scheme. I feel dirty for being used this way. I did not choose to be raped, assaulted and dragged through the streets like a dog. I would not sign up for that. For some ulterior reason, soon to be revealed I am sure, I am here entangled in a plot which I cannot see working in my favor. My life in the hands of these men have complicated things even further. I am a means to an end and this end is never going to benefit me. I am so tired of constantly being used and thrown away without regard to the cost of my personal pain and suffering. These men could have manipulated any woman they pleased. I kept thinking there was more to this. All I want to do right now is see my children. They may not want to see me after what I have done, but I am still their mother. This whole situation does not change my purpose in their lives and right now I need them more than ever.

This feeling of helplessness coupled by hopelessness is weakening my mind. I have nowhere to turn to fix what I have done. I should not have gone with these men to the house I can now call the house of chosen oppression. That was my choice and I own my choice, this is no one else's fault but my own. The reality that I am still breathing after this ordeal must mean something! If I thought they hated me, these men really detest this stranger. I hear their conversations fading in and out, something to do with the law and how this situation will cause him to also be guilty of violations. This makes no sense to me. How can they use someone who has apparently violated the law, to get someone to also violate the law? What is hypocritical is that the main man who participated in my gang assault is in this same group of men acting like he did nothing wrong. This is all so wrong. I am to be accused, belittled, embarrassed and ashamed, while the man I was with stands by with blood on his hands, my blood! These men are all the same. They all know each other's guilt but still cleverly cover each other. I have no one to cover me. All they want to do is shame me for something which was all a mistake. The sky is doing its best to cover my situation. Will I ever find someone to cover me in spite of me and love me the way I deserve to be loved? I hope that this stranger is ready for this group. I've heard that he has a very powerful presence. I think they are going to be disappointed. These heinous men constantly brag in public about their careers and families, but live lives they should be ashamed of. I know a few women that regularly visit these men privately. These women are not being paraded through the center of town like an animal without respect or dignity. What right do these men have to do this to me?

We must be getting closer to our destination because suddenly I hear throngs of jeering people, as if they were at a ball game. People are everywhere! This must be the place where the stranger is because I have heard that wherever he goes tons of people gather to hear him speak. Everyone is looking at me being dragged behind these men, wondering what in the world could I have done to be treated like this. This is quite a spectacle. I cannot believe I am being paraded like a piece of discarded, unimportant trash through a throng of chaotic people, some delighted by what they are seeing. My life is over, this public display of inhumanity is too much. My heart rate has sky rocketed, my head feels like it is about to explode and every shame, conceivable to humanity feels like a ton of weight in my life. How can this really be happening? I read the crowds uncaring eyes. I hear their vicious, uncaring and violent words. I see some smiling women that I know from around the village. These must be the wives of these men who maybe thinking that I must be the reason for their husband's infidelity. I did not seek them, they sought me. Why is it my fault? I shouldn't bear the entire weight of this mistake. I know I am sounding like a typical victim. I just heard myself and it does sound like I am blaming everything but myself. I do see my responsibility in this, but I am not alone in sharing the blame. I was not the only one there.

Quite unexpectedly, a path opens through the frenzy of the taunting crowd that I am being dragged through, and like a distant image coming into focus, I see him. I am staring directly at the stranger. He looks so calm, peaceful in fact and apparently not afraid to acknowledge me. In fact, it's almost as if he knows exactly what is happening to me and why I am here. I don't think this situation is a surprise to him. These men were excited about surprising him, but the complete opposite seems to be happening. The stranger seems ready, poised and relaxed. I on the other hand am petrified, scared and completely insane. I am uneasy because what I have been accused of is shameful. I would like to say that I have been accused falsely. I would like to say that these accusations have been fabricated and conveniently manufactured. I can only say, deep in my heart, that these accusations are unfair. I am being used. How I wish I had not agreed to deal with these men. I would do anything to have this day back, that moment back. I would absolutely make a different decision. I do not want to be here, not now! I am dragged and unfeelingly thrown before the stranger. I squint painfully as I look up through my badly swollen eyes into his welcoming caring eyes and am immediately filled with a strange awareness. The only way I can describe it is to describe it as hope. I am not as petrified as I was before. Maybe I should be, but here in this moment with him, I am not. The crowd is silent momentarily. It seems like only my heartbeat is heard above the deafening silence. I can hear the blood rushing hurriedly through every vein and vessel as if everything inside me is crying out. This is my response to the stranger. Through the crowd of men, a second group of men appear and briefly talk with the first group. I think I understand what's going on. I see the game that they are playing. This new group of men look like they have been hired to bring me to what is now developing into a hurried and public trial in front of the entire city. Very piercingly, one of the men raises his voice so he can deliberately be heard by everyone else in the vicinity. He says to the stranger that they caught me alone with a man who was not my husband. That is not true at all! They set me up! A well thought and devious plan is being presented as truth. How will I ever survive these fabricated lies? These are class action lies that I am facing. They have trumped up witnesses which I am being told is the requirement for any testimony in this town to be accepted as truth. I have been treated worthlessly before, but this is an entirely different level of treatment. They did not catch me; they deliberately arranged this situation so that they could discredit me and use me as part of some ridiculous plot. These men do not want me, they want the stranger, I mean they really want this to be about the stranger. I am insignificant to them in the sense that I am merely a means to an end. If they could have used anyone, then why did they choose me? Is there a mark over my life that attracts these kinds of men? I am feeling persecuted and targeted, and I am not understanding this. I have a feeling however, that my untruthful accusers are to be surprised. The stranger appears to be a very powerful man. This is not going to work in their favor, I pray it works out in mine!

    I just cannot spend any more time wondering about how this happened. I have rehearsed the past few days and painfully realize that I am truly not perfect, but I still do not deserve this moment. This is rock bottom for me. This is the worst that it can get. If I had to invent the cruelest punishment for my worst enemy, it would be something like this. My secret life is not a secret any more. There is no return for me. This place has scarred me forever. There is no redemption from here. The stranger has to help me get out of this. I can't turn things around for myself. Only he appears to be half way interested in handling me with any level of respect. I'm so tired of being the one that ends up on the wrong side of the deal. For once, can I emerge with opportunity and possibility? My life has always felt like a lost cause and here I go again feeling lost. Emotionally I am distraught, physically I am worn, mentally I am drained, and personally I am depressed. My life is in another tail spin and I feel wildly out of control. The fear that is attacking my mind and stabbing mercilessly at my heart is so repetitive that I can hardly breathe. I am numb from being the center of this charade and I have been slandered to the point of exhaustion. This whole situation has taken a terrible detour. I have sacrificed whatever integrity I had left to provide for my children. How in the world did I get here? This is a nightmare for me and will surely ruin my life.

2 FACING THE HATERS

The crowd is increasingly building in agitation. It seems to me that they are being intentionally incited. I hear some of the men saying to the crowd that they caught me with a man and how it could have been their husbands that I had seduced and that I need to be dealt with. I know I was wrong to be in the same room with this man, but that is all that I did. There are limited ways for any woman to make any real money in this town. There are societal things that are acceptable and have been acceptable since my childhood. What I have been doing is what my mother did and her mother before her. It is not elegant, it is not classy, but none the less it was acceptable and often ignored because it provided a service to powerful men. I am not proud of this. This is not my proudest moment, yet I am facing my haters with as much dignity as I can. I know they want to watch my demise. It is clear that the facts are stacked against me and in their eyes the evidence irrefutable and the eye witnesses all in agreement. I can only pray for what I do not deserve.

There isn't much dignity left in my shattered reputation, but I must hold on to something. It is at times like this, you contemplate your life decisions and swear that you would do things so differently had you another opportunity. I wish I had the opportunity to explore who I could have been and what I could have achieved. I might have really been something, done something. The thoughts and memories of what my life might have produced keep flashing before my eyes, but these memories are long gone. I will never be anything now, too many things have gone wrong. Now here I stand accused of something that these men are also guilty of. How come we are standing on opposite sides of this? Why is my error greater than theirs? Yet the support they have from this madding crowd is incredible. I never thought people in this village would act this way. I am looking at women that I grew up with that obviously want me to hurt. It takes a situation like this for you to discover who your friends are. Everyone has virtually turned away from me. No doubt word will reach my husband soon. My life is over. It can never be the same. The only option for me is to rely on this man who I lay here before. I really need the stranger!

I can hear these so-called gentlemen making their complaint to the stranger and basically saying that for my mistake I should be given the maximum penalty. Really! What kind of law would inflict such a harsh sentence without an opportunity for due process? Do I not get a chance to defend myself and present the facts as I know it? This rush to judgment has increased the tension of this moment and I cannot escape. I see how this is shaping up. These so-called men want to use me to entrap the stranger. I thought they wanted to just hurt me. It seems to me the outcome of both situations might be the same. They don't like the stranger. I think they want to see his reputation destroyed. They are pushing for a climactic show down but from here it seems that this is not going to be good for him or me. I hear them challenging him asking him what he thinks should be done with me. I know I should be petrified because of what is about to happen, but I have a strange feeling that if I am to be judged by anyone I would rather be judged by the stranger. It is obvious I am not going to receive any form of mercy from these egregious men. If there is going to be any mercy, any justice, any grace, it must come from someone I don't even know. I am feeling they made a grave error when they brought this complaint to him. I am sure they did not realize that they transferred this case from their hands, jurisdiction, hatred and power into the hands of a competent and skilled litigator. This I think is their greatest mistake and my chief break! I should not be hopeful but reservedly hopeful I am. I should not feel at peace, but somehow, I do. The stranger has filled me with a strange assurance that is unimaginable. Now that I am in his company, I feel I must get closer to him. This will be my only chance to come out of this unscathed. I am literally at my wits end. This is such a bizarre situation.

There is peculiarity in the way that the stranger is looking at me. It is not the same way he looks at my accusers. The look he gives them is one of sadness, disdain even disappointment. He looks as though he cannot believe the spectacle that they have created to try and back him into a corner. It is as if he discerns what they are doing. Could he be reading their motives, their thoughts? I would not put it past this man. I have heard that he can do amazing things. I need a miracle from this man. Without him I end today. Without a word from him I will not survive today. If he does not handle my case I will expire today. The look he gives me every now and then, can only be interpreted as love. I have never had a man look at me this way before. Men look at me, but with one thing on their minds. I envision their minds spinning trying to figure out how they can use me. I know that look all too well. For me it is the work look, the look that says, "if you work with me, you will be able to feed your family tonight". I have been raised to know that look, the "man look". The look that says I want to take something from you. The look the stranger is giving me however, is not that kind of look. His look says that he understands why I am here and even how I got here. There is no pretense in his eyes, no awkwardness in his smile, and nothing false about his actions. It is almost as if he is glad to see me, to meet me. He has an air of confidence about him. His look confidently says, "don't worry". I'm drawn to believe what I see in his eyes.

He does not seem bothered by the circus that these ridiculous men have caused. He does not seem bothered that they persist in challenging him. It really doesn't matter what response he gives, they are going to claim he is evading. Yet the stranger is unmoved by the challenge. It is as if he sees right through them, just like he is seeing right through me. Why isn't he afraid? All these men are gathered in this public place and there is no one here to defend him. Where are his people? This is a not a good time to not have protection. They should be here with him. I hear my name again from the mouths of these men. I cannot keep hearing my mistakes blasted in front of everyone. This is too much. I feel exposed, dirty, vulnerable and unclean. My life is stained forever and being reminded time and time again about it, is not helping at all. I am closer to the stranger now than ever before literally standing face to face with him. Up close he looks unassumingly normal. He is regular, ordinary in fact, taller than I imagined with a genuine smile. He has deeper and more meaningful facial features. I have never been this close to a man of this caliber before. A woman like me, from the worst part of town, standing in front of a man like this! I don't care too much for the circumstances that brought me here, but now that I am here, I am in absolute awe of this moment. He relaxes me even though I am mystified by him. His persona is overpowering, yet non-threatening. What kind of man is this? I have never seen anyone with this much self-confidence. I feel his peace. I am not sure why I am beginning to feel that this interaction is having a profound effect on me. I want to be a part of the peace he has. I am not sure where it is coming from, but I want it. To feel peace right now is preposterous, but peace is what I feel.

The stranger is the only one pulling for me, the only one on my side. Everyone else wants a different outcome. Yet when I am with him I am not afraid. I was so afraid before I got here and more afraid now that my secret life has been uncovered. I had always worried about what would happen to me if my secret got out. I guess I don't have to wonder about that any more. These crippling, nauseating and perplexing emotions have departed since the stranger is here. I sense something is about to change in my life, but I'm not sure what. I have never expected anything out of my life before, and I've never really had anything to look forward to. I mean what I did for a living was not a real career, or anything I could ever be proud of. I was born into a lifestyle which is all I have ever known. My mother put me to work as soon as someone showed me a little attention and when I began to physically develop. I've never hoped for anything much and seldom had anything to hope for. My life was always surrounded by abuse, sadness, pain and rejection. These memories I recall readily. What gives me the right to stand before this man, who I have never met before, and feel hope? I am surprised I am feeling anything at all. This is not an emotion I am used to. This is becoming serious. These hateful men are pummeling the stranger with one question after another and he is just staring around nonchalantly. He appears to be sizing up his opposition. He keeps looking at me with the same passive and mild appearance. He looks at me, he stares at them! The stranger is not being riled up the way they want him to be. I came screaming frantically, even cursing these men for humiliating and destroying my life. I was not peaceful. I threatened to expose all of them that were accusing me. I knew their secrets, their hidden desires. I listened to all of them drone on about their marriages and their unhappiness with the pressures of life. The stench of their hypocrisy is literally suffocating me. They had exposed my life but who is going to expose theirs? Maybe the stranger will?

    These men are sickening. Their upscale clothes can never cover up the fact that they are as flawed as I am. Just because I have no one to cover my weaknesses does not mean I am not worth something. I understand that what I do occasionally for a living is not respectable, and totally unacceptable, but what I do is not who I am. I would love to be able to try something different. In fact, I have tried to do other things. I remember, a woman in my village who was a seamstress spent time with me after my children went to school. She would talk to me about life choices. I strangely believe the invitation to learn sewing was really an excuse to get inside my head to share her wisdom and guidance. She was a wise woman. Wiser than my own mother I believe. I think she knew my mother and compassionately almost adopted this lost and desperate child. So, I have attempted other opportunities, but nothing came more naturally than what I have been shaped to do. At least I am not hypocritical like these men. I am not misrepresenting what I do. My protest is that I am not the only guilty person in this triangle. These men arranged this! Why should I be singled out while these individuals ignored? These men bullied me, but they cannot bully the stranger who is not even responding to their complaint.

The stranger is smiling and looking around. He appears to be waiting for the right moment to speak. There is no intimidation happening here. It looks like the longer this standoff goes on; the more intimidated these men become. They too have not met anyone like him. They do not know how to handle his silence. They came looking for a fight, but this kind of standoff is not what they expected. The stranger is controlling this fight. He has a strategy and he will respond, I am convinced, when the time is right. For right now it feels as though this silence is for me. It's like he is spending time with me and getting me settled for what is about to happen. I love the stranger, I just simply love this man!

3 SOMEONE NEEDS TO GET ME

Virtually I've felt alone most of my life. By that I mean, I have carried so many secrets because I could never trust anyone to share them with. To not be able to share my heart about meaningful things translates as, loneliness. I've never found anyone that could handle the real me. I can really be complicated at times. I find no comfort in the relationship with my husband. He turns a blind eye to the things that I am forced to do. To be honest, all it seems that he really cares about is that I bring home the money. We have a very unusual relationship. I thought I loved him at first, but very early in the marriage his attention turned to other things. He spent less time caring about our children and more time cavorting with the men in the village. Their daily discussions centered around the lack of respect from their wives. They eventually swapped methods and strategies for how to control women. It is ambiguities like this that has made it almost impossible to connect to him but for our children's sake, I have adjusted. He does not care for me or care about me. Why does he not stop me from this known promiscuity? He does not love me, neither does he love what I do. It makes life easier for him to ignore me and pretend that I do not exist. I can understand his emotional instability from one perspective I guess. We were forced into marriage. I was chosen for him but not chosen by him. I guess that is why it is easier for him to pretend that what I do is not important. Even though we have been joined together by marriage that is our only real connection. The abuse from him may not be physical, but I would rather be beaten than endure the mental anguish I have endured by being with him. The way he looks at me is as if what he is seeing turns his stomach. Maybe this is a constant reminder of how useless I feel in this marriage. I can't only blame him. I stopped trying to be a wife a long time ago. A slave would better describe my functionality in this home. I cook, I clean, I provide, and I care for our children. It has been an arrangement that is quite popular in these parts. All this means is that unhappiness and unfulfillment has a permanent home in me.

It feels incredibly cold when it appears that no one is in your corner. This day has dragged on and I cannot wait for it to be over. The sun seemed to hang in the sky a little longer than usual, as if to prolong the excruciating agony I'm already experiencing. Not even nature was kind to me today. What appeared to be a cool but breezy day finally turned into a sweltering furnace. I almost passed out under this oppressive heat. These were no conditions in which to carry on a long drawn out debate about my situation. Every time I felt like fainting, I propped myself up not wanting to appear weak in front of this unsympathetic crowd. The bruising in my body and the blackened swelling of my eyes continues to make it hard for me to stand. No one asked if I was thirsty or hungry even. That would be too humane a thought. There was no empathy in this crowd. If I had fallen beneath the mountain of these accusations, everyone would have been satisfied. Externally, I was trying to hold on for dear life, trying to appear strong. Privately, my chest felt tight and sore from the harsh treatment. The funny thing is I never knew I had that much strength to begin with. I must be drawing strength from the stranger because each time I feel like fainting, I find new strength to keep standing. I cannot allow this to get the better of me. It is not just the heat of the sun glaring down on my exposed head that I feel. I feel the heaviness of dishonor and humiliation. There is a real absence of forgiveness here. No one has stood to speak for me. No one expressed not one word to minimize the situation. Inside my shame my choices have convinced me that I do not deserve mercy. There are other voices suggesting all kinds of defeat, but I must stay hopeful. If I make it through this, my children will need me. I am unsure of the likelihood that my husband will forgive me, so I have to be strong for them and for me.

The beating of my lonely heart only reminds me of the beating my life has taken. I have never asked for much, but I have desired much. The little ambition I had in my youth has all faded away now. There is no point in holding on to lifeless, empty dreams. The reality is that my life is almost over. It is both awakening and defeating to face the hopelessness of these facts. I keep trying to believe that the stranger will do something to help me. No sooner than I begin to feel a glimmer of hope, immediately reality brings me back to my present prison. I am not incarcerated, but I might as well be. My end is in sight. My disgrace has already been finalized and my sentence handed down. I am free, but not free. I cannot just walk away from this hateful place. These people would never let me leave. I am not detained by chains or prison bars, but I am restrained by something far greater, my own guilt. That is the only thing that is keeping me here. Oddly enough, I'm starting to believe maybe I need to be punished. I have been bombarded with so many allegations that I think I'm beginning to believe it myself. I am losing my grip on reality. I am being used, manipulated and sacrificed. The only thing that is holding me together is the certainty that the stranger's presence can possibly be my only way out? If I could be any more depressed I would, if I could scream anymore I would, if I could be anymore repentant, I would. All of that does not change the fact that I must face this. I may not have been guilty of this latest fiasco, but maybe this is pay back for all the times I apparently got away with it. These men, these people, are drowning the very life out of me. Their ferociousness and hatred are overpowering me. They have brought me here, not to be vindicated, but to be condemned. They would plead for mercy if they were in my shoes. I cannot be broken any further. I cannot be whipped any more.

This entire situation is becoming weirder by the moment. It was weird how these men approached this man, it was weird how this whole day began, but what happened next, was the weirdest yet. The ferocity of cursing and accusing has not let up from these men. I am ready to be unconscious to this entire scene. The stranger is still unmoved and unresponsive. So, when he finally responds, I am shocked. I have been waiting for this for absolute ages it feels. So, right in front of me the stranger finally responds. In the heat of all this noise and rush to judgment, his response is not even in sync with what has been happening. I cannot believe this. He stoops down and with his finger begins to write slowly on the ground, I mean he just begins to write casually on the ground. I have never seen anyone do this before. I mean he is not responding with words but in writing. This is absolutely astonishing to everyone, more so to me. I must be honest, I too was looking for something a little more dramatic and flamboyant. This is not what this man chose to do. A collective and confused silence now immediately descends over this crowd as every mind struggles to gauge what is happening. The reaction is different with these men. I can see as they stand here that their level of fury is increasing. They have become agitated, as if insulted by the way that the stranger has responded. They wanted a verbal altercation. They did not get that. The last thing the stranger did before he stooped down to write on the ground was to glance persuasively into my eyes. I cannot be wrong; he seemed to deliberately smile, reassuringly at me. I am sure that was a smile. I know it has been a long day and I have been weakened by both the stress and heat of this situation, but I am convinced that this man just smiled at me! I must be hallucinating. I must be terribly misreading what just happened. That cannot be what he is really trying to convey.

Yes, he did smile. This is incredible, and this is why I find myself believing in him, a man that I just met. This has never happened to me before, not ever. I have good reason not to trust men at all. I have been hurt by too many lies, too much deceit and far too much abuse. I feel I can trust him. I see trust in his eyes, I see hope in his eyes, I see strength in his eyes. I wonder what he sees in me and why he looks at me this way. I know this much, that whatever he sees in me, is more than I could ever see in myself. It is not even what he sees, but that He sees something. If he sees something in me, then maybe I can become what he sees. I am accustomed to looks of disgust, despair and pity. I am accustomed to being perceived as valueless and unwanted. I understand those spirits all too well. What I am not accustomed to, and what I am surprised by, is the level of compassion and concern from the stranger. I feel sentiments erupting in my heart that I have never felt before. I'm actually feeling! I am feeling for the first time in a long time. I feel that regardless of the horrendous mistakes that I have made, something is happening right now in my life that could possibly change everything. Maybe I can change from feeling broken, useless and worthless. You see it's the possibility that I am feeling. I have no evidence or facts, but I feel possibility. The stranger has started something in me and has not even spoken to me directly. Just the way he looks at me makes me want to see myself the way he sees me. I am beginning to see opportunity. I know he heard what everyone was saying about me, but in spite of all that he stooped down to write as if it did not matter. He is showing the grace of greatness in the face of this awkward situation. I have never seen these other men, these pretentious and arrogant men ignored like this before. They are not accustomed to being disrespected of sorts. I am sure they lavish being treated with royalty and importance. They are used to being lauded and praised for their professional success in society. This time they do not have the attention or center stage. They are forced to deal with a man who stands taller than their egos and greater than their wealth. These men only talk about being great, but they are powerless in the presence of genuine greatness. If they have to hide behind false allegations, then how great can they really be? The stranger has said more about his genuineness by his handling of this ridiculous scene. So that's it, that's why they want to challenge him. Before this whole episode started, I felt like escaping, but escape where? Now I feel that I want to stand right here with the stranger and just hope that the look and smile that he just gave me means what I think it means, someone is finally going to defend me.

A long murmur resonates through the crowd as everyone starts chattering about what the stranger is writing on the ground. What an extraordinary thing to do. This was the last thing that I or anyone else expected to happen. It has taken everyone by surprise, the most unexpected response imaginable, but what has he written and who is he writing about?

The apparent show down is not going the way these men had planned. The stranger seems to be one step ahead of them. Everyone knows that the stranger is a man of peace. He never causes confusion. He is an important and influential person. Never was there violence or disruption in his presence. I think they got this all wrong. They needed a case and a cause to entrap him. Somehow, they selected me as the scape goat as a crescendo to this moment in their plan. The stranger has taken the wind out of their sails. His silence has taken over. His persona has silenced the crowd, and almost silenced my accusers. Now the stranger won't even talk to them; he won't even hear their allegations. Now who is being disrespected? He faced them, discerned them, and understood their motives. Just when they anticipated an aggressive reaction, he stoops down and peacefully begins to write mysteriously on the ground without acknowledging them at all. This thing is beginning to turn around for sure.

Just as the wind, without rhyme or reason, changes its course flowing effortlessly from east to west, this whole scene has followed suit. It has taken on an air of mystic. Now it is not clear what the outcome will be. There has been no rush to judgment. The passion of the moment has been slightly abated and, in many ways, come to a complete standstill. The amazement and confusion on the faces of my accusers is almost humorous. I know it is no laughing matter, even though I pray I will be able to laugh about this someday, but the growing sense of irony continues to unfold. All they really succeeded in doing was creating a court. When they cited the law as part of their accusation, the scene changed from injustice to inquiry. They thought by blindsiding the stranger they would control the situation and force him to make a mistake. They are now probably thinking that the worst person they could have brought me to was him. Between continued flowing fears of lowliness and loneliness I believe this entire day is playing into his strength. Perhaps that's why he is not looking concerned and being particularly nonchalant about every move that these men make. It is as if the stranger has a well-planned counter attack. You cannot beat him with the law. He is known to baffle intellectuals and scholars with his keen and creatively unique understanding and interpretation. This is getting more and more interesting by the minute and I am beginning, for the first time, to enjoy where this is going.

Why is the hope in my heart rising again I wonder? I know that I am not out of this yet, but hope is definitely rising. I can still hear fading chants of disapproval from the crowd. The chants break in like the waves of an ocean on a sandy and pebble covered shore. They want desperately to witness my punishment. If it wasn't for me standing here with the stranger, I would be more than petrified. I am not feeling that way at all because he fills me with strange but refreshing confidence. I should be fearful, doubtful and desperate. I should be frantic, inconsolable and wretched. I should be, but I'm not. I am not in denial, I don't think. I realize how this looks for me. Anyone else in this situation would be begging for mercy, screaming for their life and pleading for leniency. All around me are reminders of a choice that continues to shadow me. It's funny how difficult it is to release certain choices even in the presence of better ones. The bond that is created between what you are and what you have done appears unbreakable. Where is the path to recovery? Where does one go to apply for a new lease on life or a new beginning? This inability to find a path to a better you is tormenting enough. If I were to be thrown in prison right now, it would be far too late. Prison is where I have sadly lived my entire life. Being locked into a choice or a chosen life feels the same as being chained in prison. Yet in the center of it all, I am still drawn to refocus on the stranger. I am quietly drawn away from my own commiserations and guided to the one thing that has been constant for me throughout this whole confounding ordeal. I am not sure why I can't take my eyes from him. People probably think I am attracted to him or something ridiculous like that. I mean that is what I would normally be doing. This is different though, I think I am different now. I am not attracted to him physically, but there is an attraction of sorts, but it is deeper and more meaningful than what I am used to. He doesn't appear to want anything from me, but I am convinced he wants something for me. I hope I do not disappoint him in the end. All I have ever done was disappoint people, and this crowd, and these ridiculous men don't want me to ever forget it.

The stranger is still writing. It would help if I could read what he was writing. Literally, I do not know how to read, I never learned. I was home taught for a while but as a child, I had to work in the fields by day and help in the back rooms at night. There was no point in learning to read. I was never going to amount to anything that required that. Why waste a skill on someone that will never amount to anything in life? The things that you dismiss in ignorance prove to be vital later in life. That skill would have really helped me right now is what I am thinking. The writing on the ground continues for some time. It feels like an eternity. The more the stranger writes, the more nervous I get. Everyone is waiting to see what the writing on the ground really means. It seems now to me that the stranger is collecting his thoughts. It looks like he is writing his responses and rehearsing his statement like any good lawyer would do before making an opening statement. He is not being rushed by the importance of the moment, nor is he intimidated by the deafening crowd. He is at peace with where this is. I for one cannot wait to hear what he is going to say, if he says anything at all. I must be patient though, I must stay positive. I am begging that this is not another ruined moment of my life. The awkwardness of the moment continues until without warning, the stranger stands up abruptly. I look around, he looks at me, he looks at the crowd, and he looks back at me. It feels like he just looked through me. He pauses, smiles and prepares to speak. I could not speak. I need him to defend me. I could not think of anything that he could say that could turn the tide of this vicious crowd. Maybe it is in what he has written on the ground. Maybe that is where the solution is. What about the writing on the ground? It must mean something, there must be answers for me. What the stranger says next assuages this crowd and even, I feel, quietens the entire world. The audible gasps that are heard throughout the crowd suggests that they are also taken back by what their ears are now hearing. When I heard it, I couldn't believe it either? These were not fighting words. These were not offensive words. One moment I was the only one on the witness stand, a moment later, everyone was crowded on the witness stand with me. How powerful were these words that caused every accuser to examine themselves and for a fleeting moment divert their attention away from me? The stranger said it again and louder this time. I hear people in the crowd repeating what he said. This is what this amazing man said, "If you have done no wrong in your life then feel free to throw the first stone at her". I strain my ears to hear these words again, as if to convince myself that he really said it. I thought this was about me, but the stranger just made this all about them. It was them against me. Now it is them against themselves. Everyone knew who "the her" was. I am the her, and I cannot believe what he just said. What was it that he was writing on the ground that led to this life changing moment? I hear his voice, but I also hear his words. What he has written has changed the course of mankind and absolutely changed the trajectory of my life. I have never heard a statement so simplistic, yet so life shifting. I have never seen so many people react at exactly the same moment. For one moment, it felt like everyone existed inside the same body and experienced the impact of that statement together. There was no need for interpretation, translation or explanation. The truth of the moment seeped into everyone's heart as quickly and easily as the night gives way to day. This is not about me anymore.

The focus has shifted has utterly taken me by surprise. Instead of looking exclusively at me the crowd begin to look at themselves. I should be completely relieved but somehow not yet. I initially I feel uncomfortable about this place of transition. What happened next can only be described as a massive disorganized exodus. Everyone started leaving, sauntering out of this place, as if dismissed from a long day at school after the bell had rung. Everyone knows what it means when the school bell rings. It means the challenge of learning for that day has ended. No need for instructions or directions, everyone knows that when the bell rings, its going home time. This is exactly what is happening. I am not sure if it is what they overheard or what they saw written on the ground. No matter how it was communicated, this crowd, and these men, arrive disappointedly at the same place. What did these men see on the ground or in themselves that caused such a sudden turn of events? What caused them to instantaneously descend from their lofty perch of personal adjudication? Each of my accusers, unceremoniously, climbed down from their position of authority and dragged their own secret guilt back to wherever they lived. This is a miracle but a different kind of miracle. Most miracles that I have heard about resulted in some incredible physical healing. This miracle healed by defending me. Through these words, the miracle is that I may see again, I may walk again, and I may live again. I hear the crowd murmuring yet again, as they file out of this temporary court room. They're saying that the stranger has written on the ground the taxes that these accusers owe. Others are saying he has written about their private indiscretions and ways in which they have violated the same law they were accusing me of violating. Others are saying he has written the fault that lies in their own shattered lives and all their unknown failures. The jury is still out, but whatever they read convinced them that the allegations against me were the least of their troubles and their best course of action was simply to recuse themselves before anything else was revealed. Whatever The stranger wrote was not as important as what he said. This is the most incredible few moments of my broken life. I suddenly feel the weight of what I have lived under literally lifted from my shoulders. The unwanted spotlight is no longer on me. My life is no longer under the microscope of personal interrogation. No one will ever really be able to know the burden I was carrying or what I was going through. It is bad enough facing your private indiscretions but having to face them publicly is a level of humiliation I would not wish on my greatest enemies, not even these hypocritical men. You never know, how much you carry, until it is gone!

The stranger has lifted my unbelievable burden. So, this is what peace is. I have never sensed this before. I haven't sensed it in my home, in my relationships, or in my heart. This simple sentence from the lips of the stranger has saved me, breathed new life into me. I love this place that I am in. I love how it feels and what it does. I have much to be anxious about and certainly much to still be afraid of, but this peace thing is really nice. If I am to be honest, I have always felt different and awkward. I can truly say I have not had many days when I felt comfortable in my own skin. My life has always vacillated between despair, depression, unworthiness, unfulfillment, depravity and disappointment. That's quite a list! There have been moments when I felt like a normal person, but not enough to be significant. Everyone has challenges in life and I am no different, even though I've experienced it very differently from my world. That's why I think this moment of peace is so arresting. I take a long breath to take in this new moment in my beleaguered life. I am absolutely sure I will not have many more moments like this, so I am going to thoroughly enjoy this feeling of normality. Anxiety is where I have lived. That address has never really changed for me, just variations on the same theme. At this very moment, I feel regular, as if this is the way that it was always meant to feel. It took this situation, this humiliation, this pain to finally feel this. Why did I have to come through all of this to feel normal? Maybe there is something else in what he has written on the ground, maybe there is something that will explain why I had to endure the worst time ever to discover the best in me. By saying what he has said to this crowd literally levels the playing field and has brought everyone in this crowd, my accusers and all to the same point of realization. Money does not separate us now, prestige is not a divider, socioeconomic indifference bears no weight, we are all guilty of one thing or another. I am not rejoicing entirely. I still understand that I have been accused of something heinous, but what I am further realizing is that my mistakes are no more heinous than anyone else. These vindictive men presented me to the stranger as a problem and he transformed me into a person.

4 VULNERABLE

I am in this vulnerable place. Nothing is really settled, actually everything is chaotic. My future is in the balance and I need clarity to help me to continue to be hopeful. I'm in flux with my feelings, my life and my future. I am susceptible. I cannot determine what will happen next. All of us appreciate a certain level of control, but I am completely out of my element with absolutely no control. Who likes to be in that kind of place. This is scary for me. A thousand thoughts rush through my frail mind. I want to hope for the best, but it is far easier to cling to the worst. I find myself holding on to what the stranger has done for me, but I still do not feel that I am completely released. I could walk away now, but something else is holding me rooted to this place. This is not fear, I can only describe this as amazing hope. Something has inspired me to stay, to hold myself together and to wait. I am not sure about what I am waiting for but wait I will. If I leave, I will be no better off. I might as well stay and believe in the shift that the stranger has begun in me.

My attention, momentarily, had been drawn away from the stranger. I quickly reverted back to him only to glimpse him stooping and writing on the ground again. For some reason, I'm thinking that before he was writing about my accusers, this time I think he's writing about me. If he is writing about me then maybe there are answers here. Perhaps this is the advice I need to pull myself up from this. What is he going to say to me, what I am going to say to him? What can I possibly say to this man who has defended me without destroying me? He did not rehearse my past but inspired new vision. I am searching for words to express myself, to articulate my gratitude to him for him being there for me. I have never had anyone to be there for me. I've never known how it felt to be supported, to be understood and to be believed in. This man, before today, didn't know me, but stood up for me. This is a weird feeling. Every other man I have known connected to me contractually. They always wanted something from me. I am not accustomed to being thought of, smiled at or accepted for just me. My life has already changed just because of how this man has treated me. I have always fended for myself, always been self-reliant and self-determined. It is very strange to share something so platonic, so realistic with a man. The stranger has this ability to cause people to see what was always right in front of them. Already he has taught me that I am not the only person that has experienced a broken life. I thought my life was the only one that was an incredible wreck. In one statement, he equalized all of us causing them to see that while they were pointing fingers at me they had amazingly overlooked the huge failure in themselves. I would love to see what thoughts he is writing because he is not talking at all. The one thing that he has already said has been so incredibly redeeming; I am excited about what else is to be said. Here is the scary thing, the only person left for him to talk to is me, there is no one else left.

I believe he has more to say to me. What remains of my shattered life needs to be transformed. I stand here realizing that all I was really searching for throughout my entire life was something, some event, some incident that would offer me real change. Sometimes it takes a wakeup call like being dragged through the streets of your town for you to realize that you do have worth. I never knew the powerful effect of someone just believing in me. The way the stranger looked at me filled me with new hope and determination. It lifted me and instantly persuaded me that my life was greater than this moment. This embarrassment has opened my eyes to both new possibilities and opportunities. If The stranger could believe in me, then maybe there is something in me to believe in. I see the stranger writing words and I must hold on to the hope that one word, some of his words, if not all of his words, will help me. I have been called some ugly things by men who did not see me as a person but as dispensable property. I took it because there was nothing else challenging me to be different. Now that I have been accepted by the stranger, there is no way I can go back to that mentality. My head is clearing up. My understanding is opening. What I was doing before was not who I was, it was what I have been shaped to be. I can do better than this especially since I now know that no one that has either accused or abused me, ever had the right to judge me in the first place.

There is continued silence as I sit in anticipation with the stranger. The jeering has gone, the laughter has ended, the intensity has vanished and the threat over my life has been canceled. In this silence, I find myself grateful and thankful. The stranger wasn't directly speaking to me and yet I knew instantaneously something had to change about me. All he did was look at me with eyes, not of pity, but of compassion and promise. They heard his words, but I heard his gaze. It was a gaze that simply said this is not all you have the potential to be. This is so much greater than anything I have heard about him. I heard that he had helped people to transform their lives. He changed my life without lifting a finger. He didn't physically touch me, but he moved me. My miracle came as soon as he entered my day. Everyone in the crowd, including these false accusers were forced to examine themselves. If there is a lesson here it is that one should look inward before looking outward. The crowd's anger was directed toward me and the mistakes I had made. All they could see in me was a hopeless and lost case with no other option but to bring that failing existence to an end. When people cannot offer you a future, they offer you an end. When they have no hope for themselves they offer hopelessness to you. What I love about the stranger is that he makes you, forces you even, to see yourself for who you are. You can see yourself for what you can become because of him. My conscience being pierced is the beginning of a new journey. I had to come to this place of brokenness and desperation to understand that my conscience would not let me live any longer in a place that I had created but was not intended for me. I had to come to this place of public insult, humiliation and degradation. I had to come to this place of open shame to find my new beginning. It took something piercing my conscience to finally realize that the path I had traveled was always the wrong path for me. I had to meet the stranger to be introduced to my new reality. I cannot walk away from this moment. The one thing I am convinced of, is there is no greater place for me to be in and stay in, than right where I am! I acknowledge I am vulnerable, weak and scared, so I need strength, stability and support, so I have nowhere to go but to stay right where I am until the next step in this process.

5 **PRIVATE SESSION**

Who would have thought I would have had a day like this? This has been the most revealing day of my life. I stand before the stranger appreciative but weary. It has been a long day of emotional highs and lows. My temperament has run the gamut from the peak of tolerable, to the valley of infuriating. I have had a thousand thoughts and a thousand more regrets. I just keep playing this day repeatedly in my head. Sometimes I feel distraught to the point of collapse, other times I feel elation to the point of hope. This roller coaster from failure to faith has left me both worn, depleted and optimistic. Every time I feel that this ordeal will end, it takes another tragic twist. I keep telling myself this might work out, only to follow that thought with my confessional acceptance that I am totally guilty for everything that I am being accused of. The physicality of this ordeal is one thing. The mental pain and suffering of this ordeal is an entirely different weight. I seriously feel like I am losing my mind. I concede that I might lose my children and my husband, but also my hold on reality. The one shred of hope that has returned to my heart is the support of the stranger. I probably would have given up several hours ago if it had not been for his encouragement. I have wanted to die many times during this ordeal and only wanted to live once, when I met the stranger.

Now that I am alone with him it still remains an overwhelming and powerful experience. He is not saying much, actually not saying anything at all. I have had to deal with his silence before, so I am less uncomfortable with it now. It is like he is totally unmoved by anything that has just happened. He is not fazed by me or this scene. He is unmoved by the massive exodus of people. His demeanor has not changed; his body language remains quiet and his general attitude is calm. I, on the other hand, am still a bag of nerves, still an emotional wreck. I am still trying to rationalize and theorize this moment. I have to get myself together and prepare for whatever is going to happen to me. There is so much connected to this moment for me to be out of my head emotionally. I have to get the control back. At least I can hold my head up to face whatever judgement the stranger has for me. The greatest thing has already happened. The stranger has defended, perhaps not my honor, but my rights. I get it! I do not feel exonerated, but I feel humbled that someone believed in me enough to speak for me. It's really hard to take that all in. I am so accustomed to having things taken from me and not given to me. Yet I am standing here really not understanding how I am not receiving the harshest and cruelest outcome. He has not spoken to me again. I feel rooted to this spot, not wanting to change my position because I don't want to miss one word of my future. I like this feeling of anticipation. It's another new emotion for me and I am not quite sure how to handle it. If you give me pressure, I can take it; pain and misfortune, I can take it, but anticipation of something greater, I'm not used to that! I have lived with low expectation most of my life. I have survived with the low expectation that absolutely nothing in my life would ever get better. I expect to be hurt, I expect to be misunderstood and broken by people. It's normal for me to be beaten, abused and misused. I expect that, why would I expect anything different? Low expectation is easy living, this anticipation feeling is new. I am hanging on every breath the stranger takes, much less whatever he might say. Anticipation is teaching me that something amazing might happen for me, a shift from the past. I have had no expectation for my life, but it feels amazing to stand before this great man anticipating something greater.

Since I am depending completely on the stranger I will not make a move until he says so. I feel absolutely under his control. He has controlled me with his gaze, with his smile and with his presence. This is new. I am accustomed to being out of control, emotional and erratic. Every decision I have ever made in my life, I've always been unsure of. I have been equally as unsure about the decision as well as the outcome. I've just not been good at making choices. I am motionless because the stranger is still writing. So, this is what true leadership feels like. He has not instructed me to move. I am totally surrendered to him. This feeling is different though. I am not relinquishing control out of some level of obligation. I want to do what he says; I want to be obedient to him. This is a first! I want him to lead me and dictate the next phase of my life. He is so together. He is so poised. I am captured and amazed by his power and confidence. It is as if he knew what the impact of his statement would have and literally this court scene seems to be playing out just the way he predicted. I get the feeling that this is the outcome that he knew would happen. The statement he made about those without wrong casting the first stone literally cleared the crowd. I am here with the stranger, the man who has saved my life and I am struggling to find the words to convey to him how much he means to me. I should speak but he seems busy finishing up whatever he is scribing on the ground. I want to scream, to shout, to lose it entirely because the sense of freedom and life that I feel inside of me is simply overflowing. My accusers are gone but will they come back, will they find more men that I have been with and will I be tried all over again? I really need the stranger to tell me something, I need him to explain what happens next, so I can release how I feel.

Somehow, he must have read my thoughts because immediately he stands up and faces me again. He has that same passive but directed look in his eyes. I don't know how he does that, relax me I mean? Somehow, I know the situation isn't exactly over yet. At the same time, this silence is deafening and the thought of what will happen next is unsettling, overwhelming even. I still feel like something is missing. Maybe this is where the stranger explains to me what is going to happen from here. I feel there is very little to go back to. I can't go back to what I was or what I was doing. This wakeup call has cured me from that behavior. There are still so many questions needing so many answers and I do not have a clue where to start to fix this new emerging dilemma. Where do I go from this point in my life? I am still a mess. What am I thinking, I will always be a mess, unless the stranger can teach me something to me to help figure this out. I look at him and he looks at me and it seems like a lifetime before he opens his mouth to speak again. The stranger looks around unassumingly and takes in the scene that everyone truly is gone. He glances back and forth as if gathering the facts at the same time as gathering his thoughts. He motions for me to come closer. When he called out those who thought they were better than me his voice was decisive, authoritative and clinical. When he translated what he had written on the ground, he was instructive and directive, so that everyone understood what he meant. Now he seems like he does not want to raise his voice at all. The authoritative work appears to be done and the people that needed to be impacted have been. He opens his mouth and asks me quietly and caringly "Is everyone truly gone?"

Even though it is only the stranger and I, facing each other in the open, somehow this place has been transformed into a sanctuary. In this place, I am feeling an indifferent relief. Don't get me wrong I am appalled by the experience that brought me here, but I am interestingly celebrating the fact that my experience brought me to this destination. I do understand that the end does not justify the means, but I feel like my options have always been limited. I never felt regretful when faced by accusers but suddenly in the presence of the stranger, waiting for the consequence of my mistakes, I feel it beginning to take its toll. I begin to cry uncontrollably and regrettably. Every emotion I can think of has found its way through the stringent walls that I have set up to protect myself from facing disgrace. Every brokenness, pain, depression, doubt, accusation, protestation, degradation and hurt is now erupting out of my heart like a volcano heaving to release what has been held deep inside. Like the layers of aged lava, I am releasing layers of uncovered, unrepentant, undiscovered, untouched and unspoken realities. This is the moment I had feared. I have had to hold it together for so many and for so long. I have just realized I have been accused without being able to voice my defense. I have finally found my lost voice, the voice of my childish innocence and unearthed pain. Now that I am facing the stranger, I am truly facing myself. He is causing me to feel things I have never felt before. His presence alone seems to draw me to conclusions about myself that I have never accepted before. I have justified so much about my life. I have ratified agreements for my lifestyle which hold up in the layers of my defensive thinking but has no relevance or reckoning now that I am facing him. He is doing this to me. It was always me against them, their opinions set against my own. This is a different battle, the battle of my conscience versus the stranger's compassion. I cannot rationalize with him. I cannot compromise with him. He is way above any man I have had to deal with. Subtle gestures and soft words will not sway this man. None of my charm will find any influence. I might as well just be me and see if he can really love me for who I really am.

For the first time in a long time, I had to own up to me. Without effort the stranger has caused me to face myself. I am alone in his makeshift chamber having to change some things about me. I cannot stop the tears from streaming down my sunken face. My heart is breaking and my soul groaning now that I am alone with him. When facing the crowd, I felt anger. When facing the stranger, I feel remorse and repentance. He has brought light to my consciousness just by being who he is. I replay in my mind how these men set me up by luring me into an encounter with another woman's husband. I replay in my mind how I should have just said no and continued to try to live better. As I replay these scenes in my mind, I cannot help but weep, not for who I am now, but for the person I could have been, the person I could have become. That person is still in me somewhere, I hope. It is to this person that I believe the stranger is appealing to. The person that I am is quite obvious. It is a person who has allowed others to control and to dictate my choices. This is the path of life that has brought me to this point. If I am being absolutely transparent, I don't like the person I have become. I don't even really like the things that I have done. My motivation in doing them was to make a living, another senseless decision. Maybe this is why the stranger seems unconcerned with what I have done. He has not taken issue with my decisions or my life choices. He has not spent one-minute rehearsing the allegations with this man. It feels like he has set this aside and wants to focus on other things, greater things. He has made his stance very clear. He is a person of the future and not of the past. It is not as though my past does not have significance. The stranger simply does not hold it any more important than the choices that need to be made now. The people that brought me here could not stop talking about it, but he refused to talk about it. I am not completely convinced of what he wants to talk about, but it is absolutely clear, my past is not his agenda.

I wish I could have had a heartfelt, mother-daughter conversation with the lonely, desperate woman that I am. I would share with her how important it is to believe in yourself, and not to be defined or described by men. I would share with her the importance of understanding herself and her own self-worth. I would have challenged her to pursue education and gaining her own place in the world. I would have reminded her that personal tragedy can lead to personal triumph and that no one has the audacity to condemn you. I wasn't feeling all of this back then, but somehow, I am sensing this now. I am having positive ideas that I know I have had before but now with more confidence and faith to believe it. These are not new thoughts, they are renewed thoughts. These are thoughts that I used to have during a time when I believed I was capable of so much more. His presence is making me remember the potential that I had before someone redirected and abused my life in a sad moment of misuse and neglect. I remember that moment as if it was yesterday. Everything changed after that encounter. He was my uncle and I thought nothing of opening the door and letting him in the house even though my mother warned us never to open the door for anyone. The rest is a blur. All I know is he changed me by what he did. He ruined me by what he did. Ever since then I was drawn to men in a way that I cannot even describe. It felt like I wasted years hating myself for something I had no control over. It made me hate something that I felt like I should like. He made something ugly that I have struggled to find beauty in all my life. He punished me brutally once, and I spent the rest of my life brutally punishing myself. This is why it so easy to do what I did with this married man because in my head I was somehow re-enacting something with the hope, that this is the time, I'll overcome the struggle. I know I was introduced to a grown-up world too soon. It didn't help that my mother did not believe me when I finally conjured up the courage to share my pain. Her reaction shattered what was left of my broken heart and innocence. I did not know what I was doing. All I did was open the door. My naivety and inexperience opened the door to something far more treacherous that would affect me for the rest of my life until now!

I have not cried like this ever! I have not had anything to cry about. It is as if the stranger wrote long enough on the ground to patiently wait for my heart to begin to recognize the amazing moment that was happening. Now that I am forlorn, he motions me to come to him. His expression has not changed; his behavior has been completely consistent. When I was being viciously attacked, and accused, the stranger remained poised. When I am a complete mess teary-eyed and sad, he remains calm and relaxed. The stranger seems comfortable with my pain, my emotional storm and my moment of breakdown. He is not moved by my emotion. He understands this moment better than I do. He seems better prepared for this moment than I am. I am relieved that the mob is gone, but I'm equally as nervous standing here fighting back feelings and emotions unfamiliar to me. The anticipation at times feels too much for me, but I must be patient to hear what the stranger will say to me! Can he really fix what was done to me all those years ago? Now he speaks again with a voice mixed with power, strength and confidence. He asks me, "Where are the people that accused you?" It is as if he wants me to take this moment in. He knows the answer to the question he is asking me, but he asks me any way. Before I could even respond to him he speaks again, "Is there anyone here with any accusations at all?" Immediately he looks at me as if to say, do you see now what I have done? My eyes widen as I realize the revelation of this moment and every moment leading up to this moment. The stranger could only reveal this once we were alone together, alone in his chambers. I understand now how precious this life changing moment is. This is the moment I realize exactly what the stranger has done just for me! This is not just about this moment or this particular mistake. In this moment the stranger is fixing every mistake that has ever impacted my life. He has actually allowed me to see that no one ever had the power to judge me. Just like there is no one standing here right now to continue to accuse me, no one ever will ever again.

The stranger, is amazing. I know now everything that he has done. He has not just released me personally, he has released me forever from this horrible place. He does not have to explain what has happened. Almost instinctively I understand through his gaze what has been accomplished. To remove my accusations, the stranger had to first remove the accusers. If the accusers felt justified in the legitimacy of their accusation, then legally the condemnation and related sentence would have to be granted. There was no way to overcome all the facts of the case. The fact is that I was wrong, a repeat offender caught in the act. The facts could not be removed, they could not be explained away. This could not be expunged or cleansed. The consequence of my actions likewise could not be overcome. The act was a fact. It was a fact that I had been set up terribly by unjust men to create an unjust situation to entrap the stranger. Since the act could not be overturned, the consequence could not be erased, then the absence of my accusers meant that the accusation, no matter how heinous it was, had to be dismissed without prejudice.

I just cannot believe what the stranger has just done for me. He has set me free and released me from a consequence that I truly deserved. What mastery? What poise? What confidence? He spent all that time writing on the ground preparing that amazing defense statement. It was a classic, unbelievable piece of narration that totally took the crowd completely by surprise. It literally took my breath away to hear an argument that completely took the strength out of the tension that these men were trying to create. I thought initially the statement took the attention from me and placed it on them. It was far more incredible than that. The statement about the person without error casting the first stone dismantled the entire case. It made the main issue the least issue and made the least issue the main issue. His defense absolutely released me from the accusation and changed the accusation completely to involve everyone's error, not just my own. It is easy for people to hide behind their errors and hurl insults at others. The stranger made me feel like I was not the odd one out, the misfit. Even though I know that I am in good company with all my other devious behavior, he included them all just, so he could separate me from them all. Only The stranger!

He turns to me again. Every time he does that I feel something go through me. Every time he turns to me, I feel something turn in my life. Things are turning now; my life is turning around now. I can feel it happening. The scary thing is I still don't know what it is turning into, but it is turning. I am not concerned. I am just so grateful and so thankful that it is turning. The stranger is asking me where the people are that have accused me of horrific things. I nervously look around half way expecting to see the same people return. Everyone has gone, and they have stayed gone. In his presence, I feel the opportunity to be different. I feel like I want to stay here awhile. Whenever he looks at me with expectation and hope, I feel that my life too can have expectation and hope again. I need that after all that I have been through. I need to know that I can rebuild and that I can have a much different life. The next thing I realize is that even after everyone has left, the stranger stayed. He did not walk out with the others; he did not turn his back on me. He always faced me, never turning away even when he heard what inappropriate things I had done. They turned me in, but the stranger never turned me away. I've never had anyone do that for me.

6 THIS TURNED OUT VERY DIFFERENTLY

With the stranger it has been refreshing, a little challenging but refreshing. Challenging because, it is not that I have not confronted the reasons why I ended up in this lonely town center, with the greatest man I have ever met, but because I have never been challenged to do anything different. All I have ever known was who I am. Suddenly, with the stranger, I am entertaining what else I can be. I stand here being healed from being beaten, healing from being broken, healed from disappointment, yet hopeful that something good is to come out of this. Something good must come out of this. Even though the stranger is here, strangely enough, I feel that I am alone with myself. I have not made the time to just discover me. I have always lived for others. I realize that I have always been in a subservient, denying myself role. It begins with family and children, making sure their needs are first. I have never spent one moment before now looking out for me. I have always done what has been expected of me. When it comes to me, I finally realize I am not always good to myself. I am good at being good for others, but not good at being good to me. I am realizing that is what absolutely needs to change. I have justified my actions in the name of being good to other people. Why is it ok to be good to others but be less than good to myself? This time just being with the stranger is causing me to consider things that have never surfaced before. Considering everything that has happened and since the focus has been me, why not get everything out in the open? This is the first time in ages that anything good has happened to me. I like it. I don't necessary like the attention, but I do like the outcome. This unbelievable situation has turned my world upside down and shaken out truths that I just needed to acknowledge. One of these truths is, I just don't need to be this me anymore! The me that I am has never had a chance to be anything more. I have been a product of what I have been exposed to and have never reached for anything else beyond what I have seen. If all you see is brokenness, hurt and abuse, that is what you tend to accept as your normal. I never knew there was anything beyond that. My world and my life has been defined and shaped by these parameters. I have never dared to venture beyond what was obvious. I have never seen anyone in my family graduate from despair. That has been the limitation and curse of my environment. It is even painful right now to acknowledge that the battle that I have been fighting has been the battle of my ancestors too. I was born with this inability to succeed beyond where I am. There was never any discussion of the future. Life was always going to be this monotony of complacency and failure. If I was introduced to success, I would walk by it as if it were a stranger without shaking its hand. Where I come from, there is no other community but hurt. We have all lived there. We have all built our lives there and raised our children there. Our children have been educated in a system that perpetuates the same result. In other words, I know how to fail, and how to use the tools in the system that I have been raised in to not make life better but survive the bitterness that life brings. The stranger has given me a sense that those parameters that have defined me for so long, might be in jeopardy of being redrawn today. There might just be new horizons and new opportunities lurking just beyond a familiar parameter of pain. I can see it now. That new me is not that far away and has never been too far away. I just never had the courage to venture beyond what was expected of me, so I continued to live by the expectations of others while denying myself. What's funny is that the answer was always in me. I have always struggled with self-confidence, self-discipline and self-image. No one has ever pushed me to be better or become greater. Just this short period of time with the stranger is revealing areas in my life that will ultimately change my life.

The stranger must sense that I am still a little uncomfortable being here with him. I am uncomfortable because this is all so new to me. It will take time for me to adjust to this new way of thinking. That's just it, I never had to think before. I just acted almost robotically going through the motions of living. There was no real happiness in my day. Every day came and went with the same result as the day before. When you are accustomed to nothing, you are not surprised when nothing happens. However, something is happening here with the stranger. He has not had too much more to say which is surprising. His actions are far more meaningful than his words. His words, the little that he has spoken, have been life changing, but his actions, his unconditional acceptance of me as a person touches me in a much deeper place. It means so much to me that I do not appall or repulse him. He did not turn up his nose at me just because of who I was. I have a strange inclination that he sees me better than I see myself, greater than I see myself. There is no one to defend me except him and he has already demonstrated that he doesn't want to see anything bad happen to me. If he wanted to see me hurt, he would have allowed the crazy people that left to hurt me. I have already been hurt by life and through the process of this whole ordeal. How much more hurt can I endure? I have undoubtedly lost my family through this and more. It is a loss that I'm not sure I can recover from. My reputation, my name, my standing in this community has all been erased. You don't have to worry about rebuilding something that does not exist anymore. The stranger does not want that for me or else he would not have defended me so adamantly. His words were not fierce, not even hostile, but the impact of his defense statement was fierce. No one could quarrel with his argument.

There is more work to be done in me. I feel free from people's opinions, their assumptions and evaluations, but somehow something still feels unfinished. Something has shifted, something has ended in fact, but I feel a new phase in my life is about to begin. The anticipation is maddening. I want to be this new person I am feeling, but where do I begin to transition. The stranger seems to read my mind because what he says next nails what I am feeling. He says to me that since no one is left to accuse me, then he chooses not to accuse or condemn me either. This is unbelievable news! Before I could respond, in fact I opened my mouth to say something but what came out was the most deafening scream, my exhale of deliverance. I cannot tell you the immediate feeling of relief that I sensed when I heard those words. He chooses not to and does not accuse me either. I understand now what felt unfinished. You see it was not enough that those who tried to condemn me did not. The stranger taught me that they did not have the authority to condemn me in the first place. I know I should have the power to just move on and get on with my life, but there has been so much of this unfinished thing in me. This time I feel like I need closure to be able to put this whole ordeal in the past where it belongs. Since my new life is getting ready to start, I need to bury what has been, and resurrect what will be. The only person to help me move on is still standing here beside me.

While I am getting settled into the thinking and feeling of freedom, the stranger continues to speak to me with weightier words than before. Everything that he had accomplished on my behalf had essentially dealt with my past and my present. Dismissing the accusation and ultimately removing the consequence for my choices, has released me from a very dark space. I am no longer held by my mistakes. A very different me can come out of this, a very different and changed person can step out of the shadows. The stranger speaks again and this time his words are more directed and challenging. There is a shift in his tone. He is a little more assertive, a little more intentional. With a more authoritative tone he calmly says, "Leave this place and don't do what you did anymore". I had to pause for a moment and let those words sink in. This is the only time that the stranger has come close to even speaking about my mistake, but he only mentions my past, to segway into my future. The stranger does not want to bring me back to the pain of what happened because I am sure he wants to see me in the light of a new day. I get it now. This is what I really needed. I needed to walk away from this place totally free. There is no question that this is what I needed. This was the final piece of my release for me. I did not take the charge from the stranger negatively. I took it positively. How could I have anything but gratitude for the only man who defended me in my time of crisis? This is still uncharted territory for me and I am still wanting to believe that a man could really love me this way. What would I ever have to say negatively, to the greatest man I have ever met? I deserved worse than a stern charge. It took this last statement from the stranger to release me to new life. The stranger did not just say that he did not condemn me, but he concluded with a statement of expectation for me, as if he believed I could do better. I feel life running through my veins. I feel strength returning to my tired and weakened body. It is amazing what hope will do. I am weaker that I had previously thought. This has been such a long ordeal and I am surprised at my mental and physical stamina. I did not feel defensive by my verbal challenge. The stranger told me what I was without making me feel like I was it. He allowed the obvious to be obvious, but pointed me away from what I was, to what I could be. I could not become anything greater if I was simply going to keep doing the same thing that brought me into this situation in the first place. I could not keep giving myself away to people who cared less about who I was and more about what they wanted. I want more for myself now. These other people were only interested in the gratification of the moment. All they cared about was their own personal needs being satisfied. There was no future in that lifestyle for me. The stranger, with his compassionate words gave me a future.

My future began with these words, "Go and don't do it anymore". He did not categorize my faults or make me feel worse because of the type of fault I had been engaged in. He did not use the occasion as an opportunity to diminish me. The stranger set me free. He gave me a point of reference. He described my past and defined my future. This was my turning point. Deep in my heart I had longed for things to change but did not know how to end the vicious cycle of despair I was in. This merry-go-round of painful indecision coupled with hatred and self-destructive tendencies was destroying any life I had left. I just need this season in my life to be over, I needed a new beginning. I needed this kind of start. Any other outcome would have left me still wondering if I could ever live beyond this place. The feeling that it is over has overwhelmed me. It really is over. The lifestyle that I could not break free from is actually over, and all it took was a word from the stranger. He told me to just stop doing it. He spoke it like he knew I could do it. I can do this. I am capable of walking away. Being controlled by men was all that I knew. I did it well for so long. Clearly the stranger believes I can do other things, but to do other things, I must stop doing this thing. This thing has used up all of my talents, all of my energies, all of my gifts. How would I know if there is anything else that I can do if I never try something new? I feel empowered to do something different. Only the stranger could breathe new life into me. He gave me back the life that I had lost. The stranger saved my life and then gave me back a life equipped with new opportunities and possibilities. His words keep ringing in my ears and resounding in my heart. I can go; I can leave this place with the power to not do the things that brought me to this juncture in my life.

This is not just a juncture in my life, but this has been a stronghold in my life. I am overjoyed that I can finally leave what I have been stranded in for so long. I have cried in this place and no one has heard me. I have done some awful things; even the men that I did those awful things with did not hear my cry. I felt like no one ever cared enough. In the absence of a path to change, I simply continued to do the things that came naturally. It is from this place that I am willingly and joyfully leaving. I am not leaving with the anxiety of returning but leaving with the anticipation of an empowered life different than the one I have lived. I am going from this place not with the memory of what I was, but with the peace of who I am. There are some things, however, I will never forget. I will never forget the man who saw me and still loved me. He saw everything that I had been but kept searching for everything I could be. I will never forget his voice, the voice that launched fresh desire. It was his voice that convinced me that this was it; the thing I had only dreamt about was possible. I will never forget his words that seemed to cleanse everything that had stained me. I literally felt all the dirt and filth that I had built up over the years finally rinsed from my existence. No more would I be defined or described by what I had been through, I would now be defined and described by how I came out. I am coming out of something awful into something awesome. I will never forget the tone in his voice and the look in his eyes. The energy that I felt being alone with him will forever be etched in my heart. I have never been alone with a man before and been so relaxed. I was relaxed but apprehensive about what to expect. This was a very special moment in my life, a time that I would never, thankfully, forget. I wanted to stay in this place to sustain this feeling. I am experiencing freedom in an entirely reformed way. I have never known this. It is like I have been reborn in a world in which I get to make different choices, better choices. Everything that I was is being left in the womb of the past, and I am being ushered into a brand-new world to, as the stranger stated, to do it no more. No more me is such a transformative thought. I get to start over and get this, start over in the place that it all began. I don't have to move out of town or relocate to another village. I feel empowered to begin my life again amongst the people that may still despise me. This is the power of what the stranger has enthused me with. I can be powerful in a place that disempowered me. I can be new in an old system. I get to choose what kind of life, purpose and existence I want to have. The power to leave this place, rejuvenated and restored is complex in ways, and simplistic in others. I still must deal with the attitudes of those who have not changed and will not change their opinion of me no matter what. This is not going to be an easy transition, but I am ready to live out my new purpose. There are so many things I am not going to do anymore, oh, but so many more things that I am now prepared to try. My family get to have a new me. My children get a new mother, my husband, if he still wants me, gets a reformed and faithful partner. If I could successfully trade in infidelity, I am sure with this fresh start, I can find a profitable trade to build. There is an empire in me, a movement that I am committed to promoting. I have received help, and now I can help other women who are caught in the same vice. My new work will describe the new me. The new me will define what I do, which has been a missing element for me. The emptiness has been filled with fulfillment.

That's right, I am not going to make these kinds of destructive decisions anymore. I am not going to put myself in situations that control me, only the situations that I can control. I am worth something more now. I know my worth. If the stranger believes in me, and trusts that I will take full advantage of this new place that I am in, then I am not going to disappoint myself or him. I can never come back here to humiliation. I have faced myself for the first time, and even though it's an awkward and painful look, I will not see this person again. It does not worry me how others perceive me. They will have nothing to judge because I will not be living in the lifestyle that brought me down. I am moving from here, renewed and revived to take on a world that is still hostile, still judgmental but, the difference is, I am free. The haze of hopelessness has been lifted by this amazing man. His words, although soft and reassuring, carry life and promise. His words are stacked with truth, compassion and responsibility. "Go and don't do it anymore", is what he said. Go and don't do it anymore is what I will do!

When he spoke those words, I felt the chill of conviction and the power of resurrection all at the same time. The chill of conviction because I understood that I got caught up in a thing that engulfed me. The chill of conviction because I know I deserved to be discarded. Maybe the conviction I was feeling was a recognition that there is a different me emerging. Maybe conviction is God's way of reminding me that there is more to my journey and my life. This has just hit me. I get the opportunity to redirect this generational tendency in my entire family. This has also got to be part of my journey too. I get to teach my girls how not to live their lives trapped by this inner struggle with men. The power of conviction is simply reminding me that sometimes being the me of the past is not good enough to make a difference in the me of tomorrow.

The stranger makes me feel the power of resurrection. I sense something new rising out of my old existence. I believe my rise is an indication that my falling days are over. Because of my desperate cries for help, my children and I have been rescued. This place called resurrection is such a powerful place. This place called resurrection is not where you are destroyed, but where you are empowered. This painful process that I have been through somehow did not destroy me, but it has developed something much more in me. I am beginning to understand the process that I had to endure. It has been a long journey of learning myself, through the mistakes I have repeatedly and consistently made. I am delighted in a way because it has led me to this point of healing. When you have had enough of what has been daily pain, you learn tolerance, but you also learn frustration. I am now in a place where my frustration has triumphed over my tolerance and I want to be different. The stranger did this for me! I can walk away from amazing uncertainty to certain freedom. I get to rewrite how I am to be remembered. There is no one left that can cast judgment. The stranger made sure of that. Everyone knows that we all have our own hell that we all live in. My hell was made public, the crowds suffered hell in private, but hell is hell. I get to walk out of my hell with confidence today. The sentence I deserve has been expunged forever. Now I get to move ahead, in spite of the things that I have been hurt by. I get to live again!

This is an incredible turn of events for me! My life was in his hands and he held me together. My entire future was hanging in the balance between people who had everything to say about me, but didn't know me, and a man who said little about me, but knew everything. It was touch and go there for a minute. I was accused of everything but the one that mattered most, accused me of nothing. Can you imagine how I was feeling? Everything was being thrown at me, but with the stranger, I survived. Lie after lie, accusation after accusation, insult after insult and all the stranger did was stoop down and write on the ground. It was not what he said that turned the tide, but what he wrote. What he wrote was more powerful than anything that could have been said. I never understood his strategy, but he did. The stranger stood between what I was and what I could be and fought for that chance for me to experience that what I could be. The stranger hung in there long enough with me to give me the opportunity for be forgiven. My life was in his hands and the fact that I am still here is proof positive that the stranger came through. Don't judge me!

ABOUT THE AUTHOR

PJ EDMUND, Sr. has published several books including: Walk With Him (Managing Your Call to Ministry), Principles of Effective Leadership, Be Positive (Keep A Word of Faith in Your Mouth), and Failure Did Me A Favor. He was born in Bristol, England (UK) and is a Bishop in the Lord's Church, founder, president & ceo, and senior pastor of Timbrel Churches International, Inc. one church in two locations (Largo and Baltimore) based in Largo, Maryland (USA). PJ Edmund is a multi-gifted speaker and author, and training and business consultant. He also serves as the General Overseer of Pneuma Fellowship of Covenant Churches of the Apostolic Faith.

Made in the USA
Columbia, SC
28 June 2024